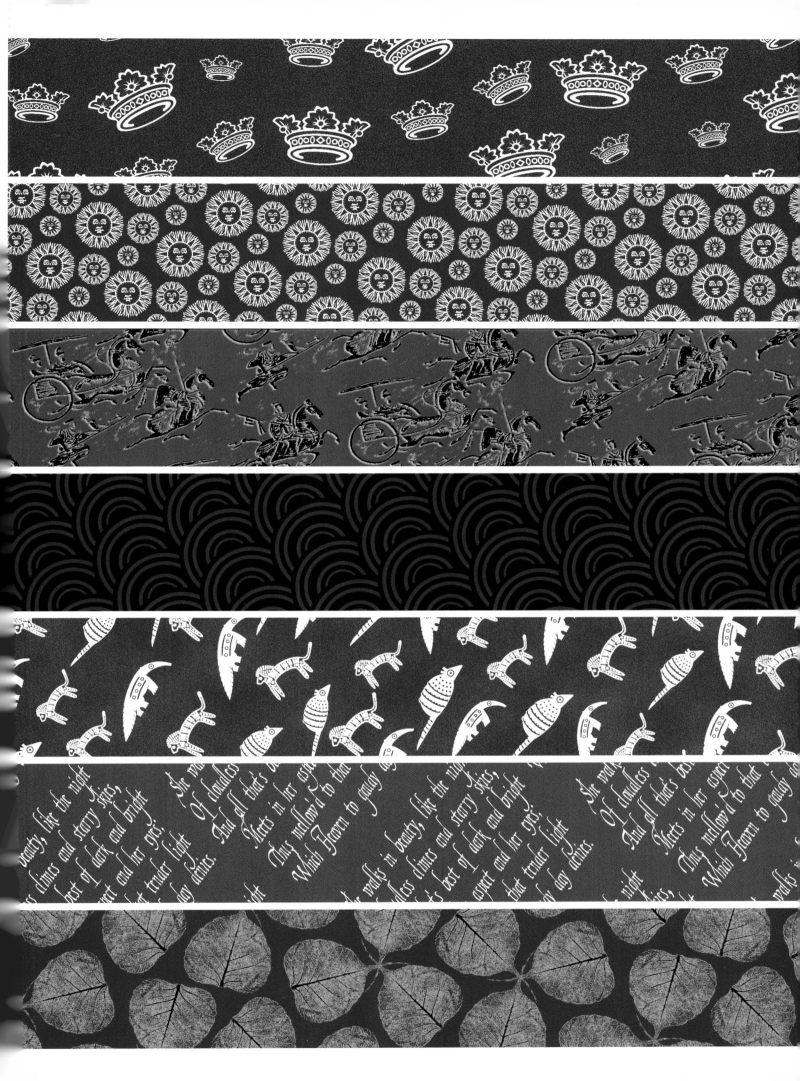

pipes, play on;   Fair youth, beneath the trees, thou canst not leave   Though winning near the goal—yet, do not grieve,   Heard melodies are sweet, but those unh
more endear'd,   Thy song, nor ever can those trees be bare;   She cannot fade, though thou hast not thy bliss,   Are sweeter; therefore, ye soft pipes, pla
o tone: Bold Lover, never, never canst thou kiss,   For ever wilt thou love, and she be fair!   Not to the sensual ear, but, more endea
thou canst not leave   Though winning near the goal—yet, do not grieve;   Pipe to the spirit ditties of no tone:
se trees be bare;   She cannot fade, though thou hast not thy bliss,   Heard melodies are sweet, but those unheard   Fair youth, beneath the trees, thou cans
nst thou kiss,   For ever wilt thou love, and she be fair!   Are sweeter; therefore, ye soft pipes, play on;   Thy song, nor ever can those trees be b
goal—yet, do not grieve;   For ever wilt thou love, and she be fair!   Not to the sensual ear, but, more endear'd,   Bold Lover, never, never canst thou kis
                    I heard melodies are sweet, but those unheard   Pipe to the spirit ditties of no tone:

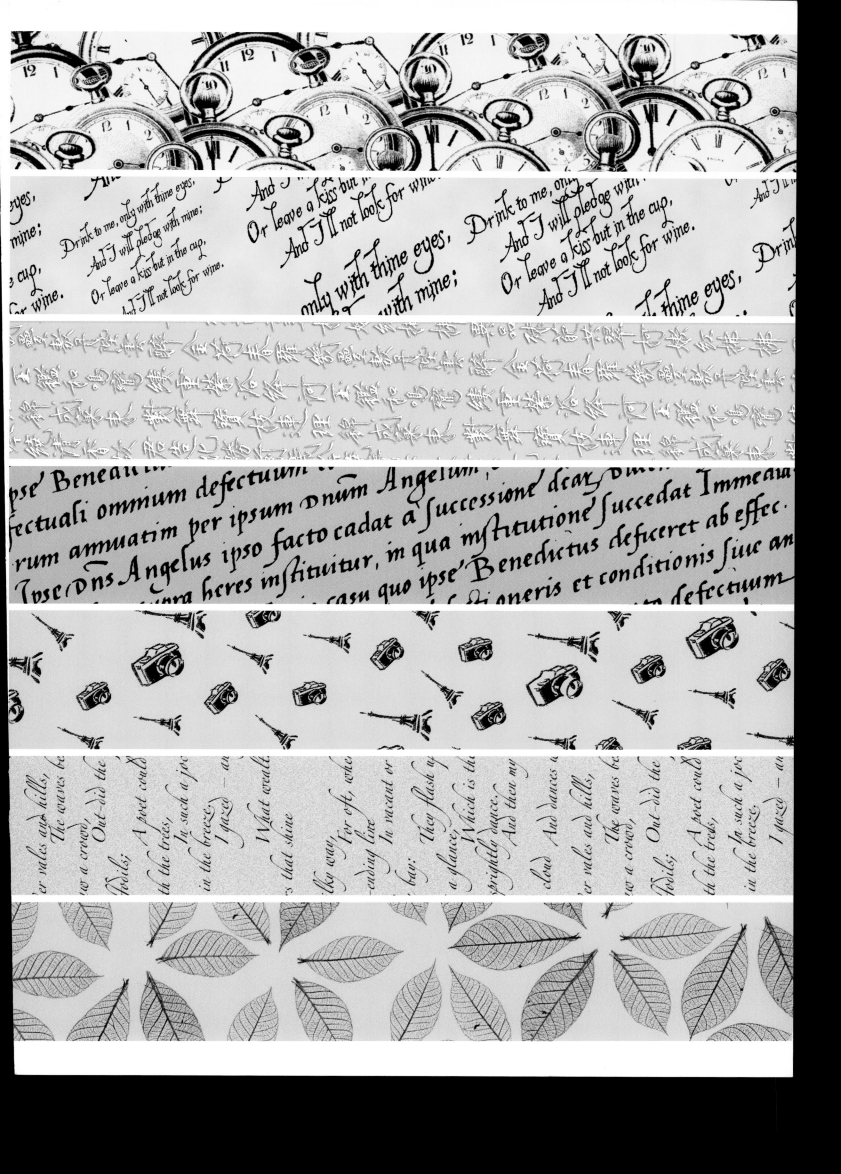

She walks in beauty, like the night
Of cloudless climes and starry skies,
And all that's best of dark and bright
Meets in her aspect and her eyes;
Thus mellow'd to that tender light
Which Heaven to gaudy day denies.

pipes, play on;
nore endear'd,   Fair youth, beneath the trees, thou canst not leave
o tone: Thy song, nor ever can those trees be bare;
, thou canst not leave   Bold Lover, never, never canst thou kiss,
se trees be bare; Though winning near the goal——yet, do not grieve;
st thou kiss,   She cannot fade, though thou hast not thy bliss,
goal——yet, do not grieve;   For ever wilt thou love, and she be fair!

Though winning near the goal——yet, do not grieve,
She cannot fade, though thou hast not thy bliss,
For ever wilt thou love, and she be fair!

Heard melodies are sweet, but those unheard
Are sweeter; therefore, ye soft pipes, play on;
Not to the sensual ear, but, more endear'd,
Pipe to the spirit ditties of no tone:

Heard melodies are sweet, but those unh
Are sweeter; therefore, ye soft pipes, pla
Not to the sensual ear, but, more endea
Pipe to the spirit ditties of no tone:
Fair youth, beneath the trees, thou cans
Thy song, nor ever can those trees be b
Bold Lover, never, never canst thou kis

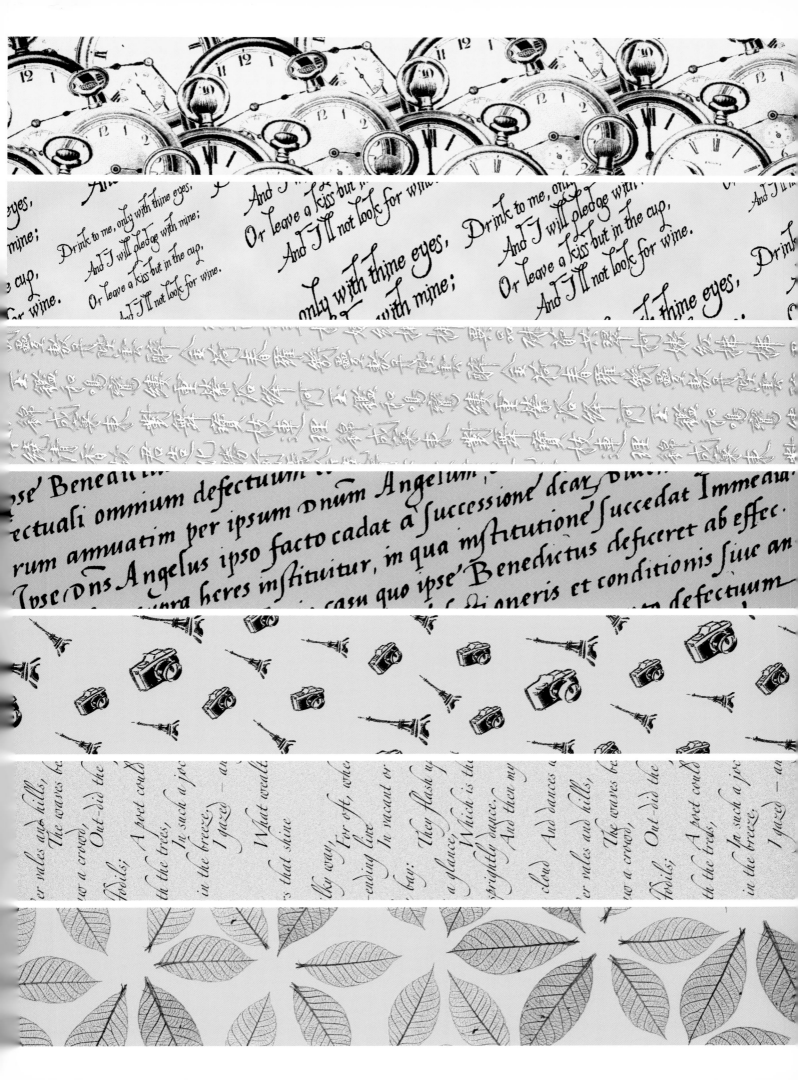

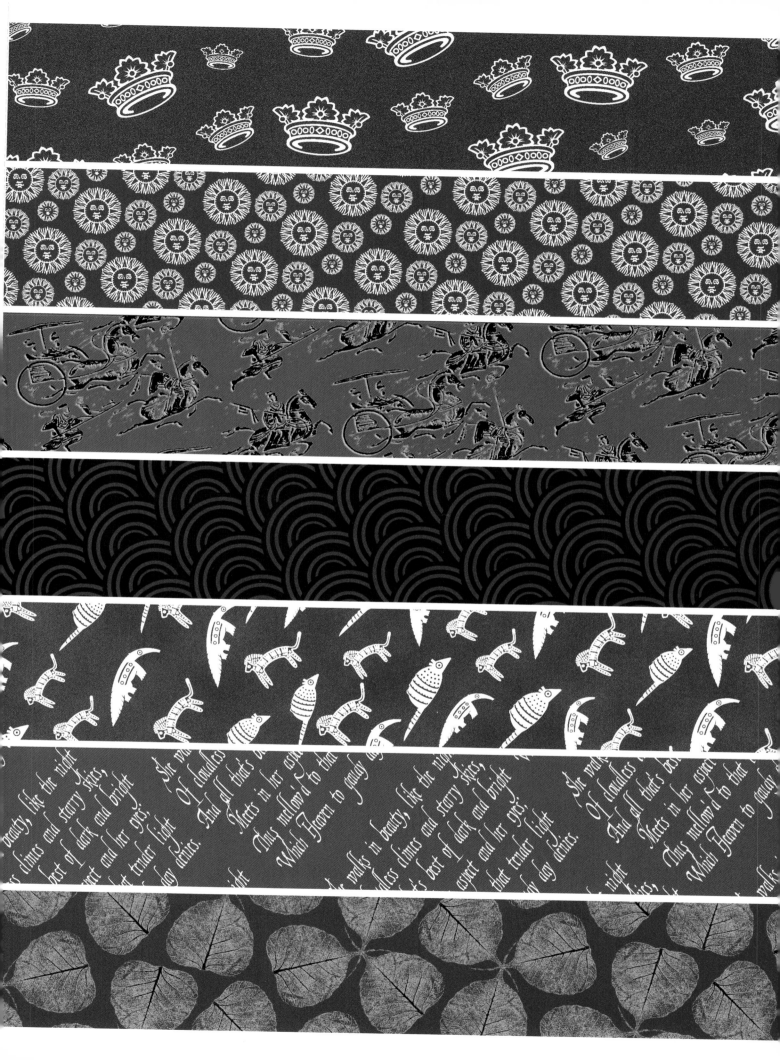

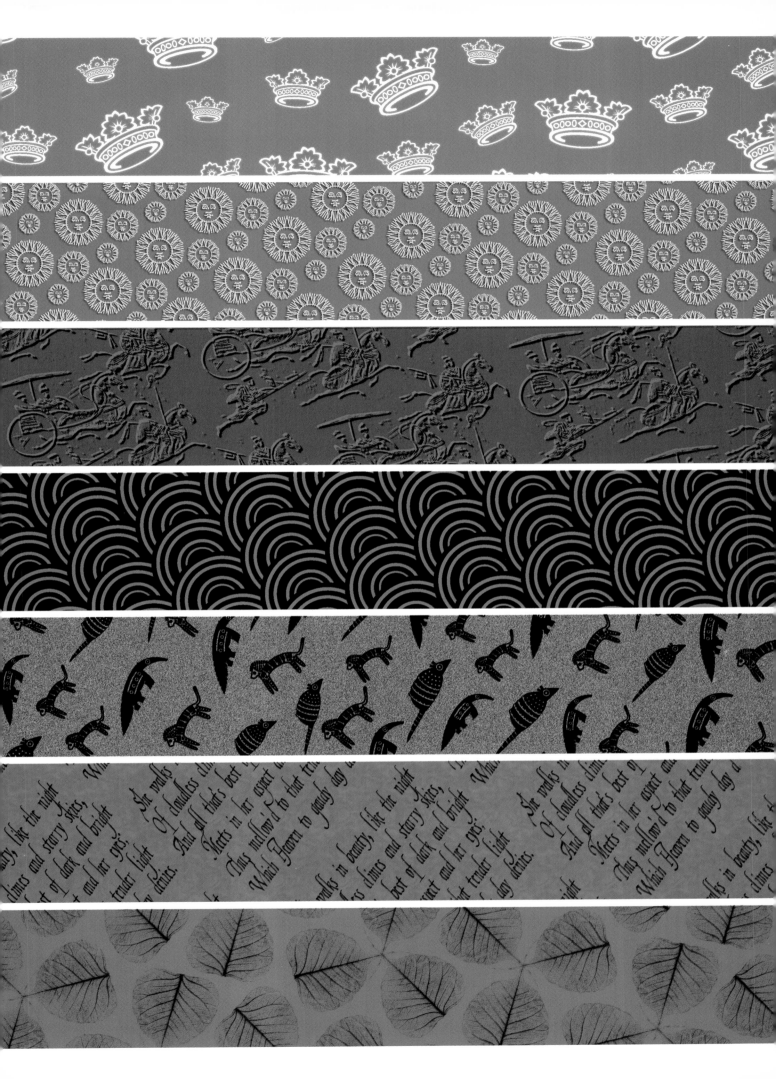

soft pipes, play on;   Fair youth, beneath the trees, thou canst not leave   Bold Lover, never, never canst thou kiss,
, more endear'd,   Thy song, nor ever can those trees be bare;   Though winning near the goal—yet, do not grieve;   Heard melodies are sweet, but those u
no tone: Bold Lover, never, never canst thou kiss,   She cannot fade, though thou hast not thy bliss,   Are sweeter; therefore, ye soft pipes, pl
es, thou canst not leave   Bold Lover, never, never canst thou kiss,   For ever wilt thou love, and she be fair!   Not to the sensual ear, but, more ende
ose trees be bare; Though winning near the goal—yet, do not grieve;   Pipe to the spirit ditties of no tone:
anst thou kiss,   She cannot fade, though thou hast not thy bliss,   Heard melodies are sweet, but those unheard   Fair youth, beneath the trees, thou can
e goal—yet, do not grieve;   For ever wilt thou love, and she be fair!   Are sweeter; therefore, ye soft pipes, play on;   Thy song, nor ever can those trees be
             I find melodies are sweet, but those unheard   Not to the sensual ear, but, more endear'd,   Bold Lover, never, never canst thou k

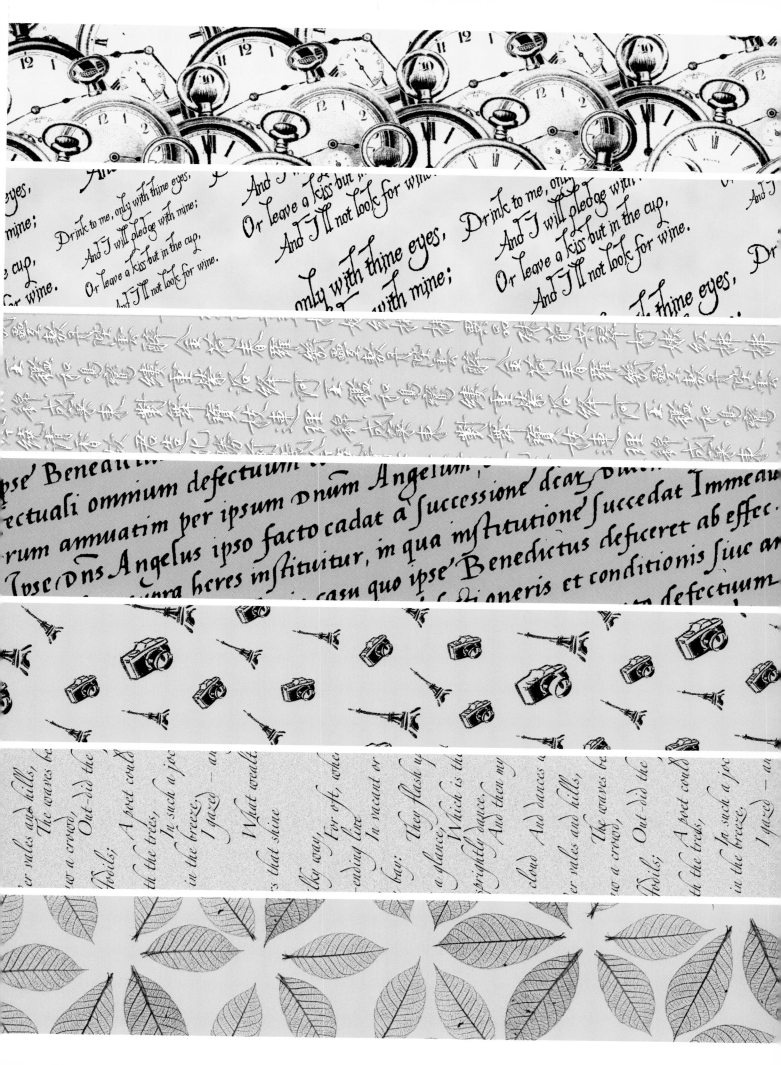